Four

beautifu
l days

Insha
khan

Meerut Sunday morning in rajput is always the great as the sun and the moon but today the it is a disaster happening in our house.

When i was eighteen years old, i want to travel Kolkata, reached every area and the corner of that city. But i have a mother, who thinks if i travel Kolkata, i will be lost or may be someone kill me. She is underestimating my love from the city.

Yesterday night, I told my mother about Kolkata but she refused on my face even yell at me too but today morning, i will make her agree at anyhow and most probably my nani, is with me. I sit on the breakfast table, my nani and mama too, we all were eating breakfast, eating omelette with bread. I started the conversation with saying ‘mama can i go’, my nani was also started saying ‘make her go n...why are you being devil of her dreams’. And my mama said with caring voice ‘if anything happens to her?’ my nani replied with angry face ‘she is the granddaughter of rajput’s no one can ever touch her’. My mama loses the argument and she walks away. My mama she loved very much but she cares more than loving me, my dad and mama separated many years ago, when i was in high school, from then she cared for me very much and scared of loosing me

I was wishing from inside that she will be say yes and then i go to nani room and she said with smile, i made up your mama mind, she is ready for you to go Kolkata, i was very excited, i call naina and tell her first about my Kolkata, she is my best friend, she lives in our house with rent. After knowing these, i booked my tickets, i started packing my clothes, even I take naina with me for shopping.

After Sunday with excitement, i wake up for office my mother was still, upset for me but while we were eating breakfast she tell me that 'she invited Akash and naina for dinner as Akash birthday is there' Akash live in out rajput mansion with rent and my mama likes him very much, she adores him like his own kid. I was being very late so I leave for the office.

I reached on my office with McDonalds burger and four cappuccino coffee hang on my left arm, the elevator was struck, I was stood on the reception but that's not irritate me, I take stairs. It is very hard to take stairs from ground floor to fifth floor, but my happiness ignores the shit. After climbing very high, I reached on my floor, I said a 'hiiiiii..' for so long, everybody looked at me with annoyed may be, I was looking very weird.

Lucky: what happened to you?

Ria: it seems like, she is happy; but why?

Ria and lucky my great colleague's they sat nearby me , so become friends. Ria is very good, she talks cutely, she eats, she work even she walks cutely, every boy had a crush on her except lucky and yash.

Me: Any guesses

Lucky: are you dating someone

Ria : no, she cannot

Me: shut up

Yash: she is going Kolkata on a solo trip

Yash my buddy since college, in college we were not that great friends but we were in same group after having same placements in office, we become best friends, he know everything about me even he is first person I called him for telling good news.

All together: whoa!

Me: After two days, you cannot able to see me

Ria: When you will come?

Me: after two weeks

Lucky: oh, two weeks will like heaven in this office

Me: hey.. (everybody laugh)

I was wishing inside, is all will happen good or not? But before that I want to enjoy the moment.

After a heavy day in office, I went off to go back home. I was bit late for attending dinner with my neighbors. I booked cab fast and sit down on cab looking the building and house thinking that “meerut is developing day by day but people re same as 90’s , some ‘haveli’are not reconstructed yet, five to ten families still are living there but still they fight like childish after all it is India nothing changes fast”

I arrived home after some time, I knock my own house door, naina open the door with smile, I hug him for the moment and she whispered me in ears “your mother will kill you”

It was akash sitting on our sofa drinking coffee, he stand for welcome me. He was a perfect boy, his looks, his family background, he lives near our house but his family belong from ‘sarpanch’ and they are very rich. My mama wants me to marry this perfect boy that is the reason she held dinner for akash and he thinks my mom is very nice but she is selfish.

He looked at me and I say “hey. Happy birthday” we both shake our hand and my mom is smiling beside. My mom grabbed my clothes and takes me to the kitchen. I asked “what”. She says looking outside “look at the naina, look at her dress.”

“Mama, I am looking independent woman in this”

“I can cancel your Kolkata trip”

“This shitty clothes, I hate this mama, I will change this”

I wear a white frock suit may be this will look better on this dinner and my mom will be happy too. I walk out from my room wearing left earring. I look over the dining table, dal makhni with tandoori roti and fried rice also salad with great plating. The smell and the plating was all good ‘dhaniya’ kept perfect on the top of dal makhni.

We all sit on the chair, I was sitting in the middle of nani and naina on front mama and akash was sitting. I serve plates to everyone and put dal makhni, when it was turn of Akash, my mom was smiling so I say “you can take by yourself” my mom smile turned to angry face and she say “hey”. As a perfect boy and chilled boy he replied with smile "she is my good friend, she can joke". I smiled at looking at him. Naina and nani ma was smiling too while looking at me.

We all start eating and gossiping about our lives and then the Kolkata topic started, my mama started telling the story about how I convinced her, how I was in a bad mood and my mom was angry too. He replied with smile "I like your guts, you are very brave" before I was replying, my mom tell him that, when I was eighteen I want to go for study at jaipur but she refuses, and he replied "may be she does not like meerut" and again before I was saying anything my mom again replied "yeah", then naina said "she likes meerut but not the rituals of uttar Pradesh". I looked over naina with smile. My nani ma does not like akash , she think he is boring because he is, but we both don't know why mom like him that much. My nani whispered me in his soft voice "yeh ladka mujhe bhaut pakka ta hai bittu, isa bol jayen yeh apna ghar par" this line makes me laugh, but I was laughing very badly from inside.

The dinner was finally get over, we all says bye with giving best wishes to them. I was lying down on my bed, switch on the laptop, I booked the tickets for departing Saturday. I open my wardrobe; take out the travelling bag and some sort of dresses that already get selected for Kolkata's destination.

(two days ago)

I wake up in early morning at 6 am, the 'Pooja' was going in my house, the voice of bell wake me up. I picked up my blanket, I walk away from my room. My nani and mama doing 'Pooja' for my safe trip. I shout at them "what is this?" then nani looked at my mama and says "ab bittu uth hi gyi hai toh isa pooja m bithal de" I replied them with annoying face "my flight is there on 10, I want to sleep and you all guys are doing this" nani harshly said "tera Kolkata jana cancel kradungi, duptta le kar aa aur beth" with annoy face, I sit on the pooja and pray for my safe trip.

After having a 'pooja' I started keeping some cosmetic, accessories and my useful documents. Then my mom enters on my room with a plastic bag, mama give the plastic bag on my hand and say "this is 30,000 rupees keep them safely". I looked on the bag and i looked on her eyes, I give her back and say "I don't need of this, I have my enough saving; save this for buying a car"

"hey, take this"

"if I had to travel Kolkata with your money, I visit many years before; according to my principles I had to travel Kolkata with my money"

"Now, you are a strong independent woman"

She hug me with kiss me on my forehead, I again hug her with strong smile. While she was going away from my room, I said "mama, I will be safe".

It was 9:30 am, my flight will get depart at 10, my mama packing some food and my nani was standing beside, she was squeezing my palm. I open my door for leaving, my mom voice came from behind take this (alooparatha). I came out standing on the stairs, she came and look on the other direction , I turned my face on that direction. Naina vegetable bag fall down so, Akash came to help her that make my mama jealous. I smiled for a bit just then she hit me on my back and telling me to force in between them. 'It will be look weird'

'I can locked you in your room and your flight will be miss'

'I am going' with making annoy face, I stand near by them and I tell them I am going off after half hour. They give me smile and wishes for my safe journey. Naina hugged me and akash put hand on my shoulder, then my mama came with rush and says 'saira, how you will go' with quite nervous 'with cab mama' 'but still, anybody had to go for saying bye'. Then, akash suddenly says with confidence ‘I will drop her, aunty’, ‘yeah…’. I was thinking silently that my mama is very genius in this sort of things. I said with sweetly ‘no, akash it’s okay’. ‘aunty, is saying correct someone had to drop you airport’

I had to get agree with my mama. It was all silent in car, I was looking at a sky and thinking, how I will manage, I will be safe or not. Anyway, it will be fun.

‘hey you are cool, everybody scared for going in a big city but you’ he hold and I replied ‘it is not scared for everybody, some people love to being scared’. He looked at me and say ‘you are very different from girls’. I also looked him with the same expression as his ‘every girl in this world is different, from how many girls you had said this line’. He smile looking at steering ‘very, few’.

After having boring conversation, we reached on airport. He opened the car trunk, I take out my suitcase. I told him to leave, he says bye and take care and left out. I was thinking, if he want to be my partner, he had to come inside and help me for check in the airport.

After having some sort of formalities, I sat on the airplane. The best thing, I sat on the window seat. The plane was not started yet but still the sky, the sun and the crowd was looking beautiful in the window. I know that I will reached after 3 hours but still, I was nervous may be it is happiness or may be something bad is going to happen. It was all in my mind so, I closed my eyes for bit. After some minutes, the plane was started, I closed my eyes and rembering a 'lucky ali song (safarnama). I opened my phone and connect my head phone, I switch on the Spotify for listening (safarnama), for one hour I was continuously listening the songs. My head nerves become collapsed, so I take a nap. The plane land softly, the pilot was perfect. All my internal organs shouted 'we are in kolkata'. The enthusiastic saying to jump all over but my manners stopped.

It was cloudy whether sky was looking perfect the colours all over looking joy, it seems like every colour is waiting for me and now, it is welcoming me. The sun was perfect in the position, the crowd was smiling, laughing, being angry or irritate but not sad. That is the reason the Kolkata called the city of joy even in the smell of soil in the Kolkata is felling joy. I wish this city will never lost its joy.

I take exit from airport, there were many yellow taxis standing outside , many drivers were standing and giggling when I walk towards them all gather around me and telling me to sit on their taxi, just then I took my phone from the bag, that was hanging on my shoulder, I switch on my phone and search on Google about best hotel in Kolkata, the holiday inn was top on the list also it was in my budget. I ask one of the drivers to drop there, I bargain some of them and I sat on the low budget taxi. I open the window slights to look the building but my hair started flying so , I thought to tie them but I look over my bag, it was nowhere, I look down on the seat even in the driver and the passenger seat but it was nowhere, I asked the driver to help me, he also search for everywhere in the car but still we cannot find anywhere but then he tell me 'madam yeh Kolkata hein, yha acha logo ko dekh kar bag hal chori ho janta hein'. I asked with quiet nervous that 'please turned the car toward airport'.

We reached airport after some minutes, the crowd was same like we left but my nervousness causing irritation this time, I beg every driver, if he had taken my bag but they were refusing. The increase of minute failure my heart, I was stuck with crazy situation; I don't even know my bag stolen by someone or lost by me. I don't even know where I had to go, who will help me, I am dying with thirst and starving. The weather was being sunny so, I walk inside the airport and sit on staircase with squeezing my arm, my suitcase was standing beside the load was looking very heavy as I lose the strength.

I looked around the people, there were many people who were getting happy to meet their loved ones after so long time and somewhere there is people who are sad for saying bye to their loved. There are many people who lived with long distance relation but here I am who did not lose person but the money, increasing of seconds making me scared, regret, tears, frightened, angry and sad.

I am scared what if I had to spent my night here, what if I had to spent my whole life stuck in this airport, that is very bullshit that cannot be happen. It is half n hour with thirst and starving and missing my mama badly and then suddenly a voice came 'it is Kolkata police you are under arrest, if you want to hire a lawyer you can' that bold gives me strength again. I stand and rush towards that voice with leaving my suit case; I looked at him they were three members with white uniform and the suspect that walking with handcuffs between them. I stopped for minutes and take a breath and shout 'stop please stop' but they unable to listen then I raised my hand and started rushing towards them and suddenly someone grabbed my shoulder and push from behind. It was a man in the age of 27 and 28 wearing a denim shirt, his face was little bit fair but his nose was very sharp and the eyes was swallowed like, he did not sleep for nights and his beard was looking amazing at him although he was handsome and some sort of cool, now back to the encounter that is happing in our eyes. I left my elbow with jerked and turned around to look police officer but he again grabbed my both elbow and said ‘your, boyfriend is a criminal, you have to open your eyes’ he hold his knees and look down ‘don’t call any lawyer, it took me 7 days and nights to catch him’ adding that, what is that, he is thinking that I am suspect girlfriend holy shit! I replied with rotten eyes ‘that is the misunderstanding, my bag is stolen or may be lost so, I don’t have money and phone; that is the reason I rushed towards police officer’ I hold and look behind the police officers but they had already left that makes me loose the temper and I shout at him ‘because of your misunderstanding, the police officers left and I don’t even know where is police station’. He was yawning and rolling his eyes it is seems like he was ignoring me, he turned back and look on the staircase, where I was sitting than he said 'do you want to lose the suitcase too'. I also look over the staircase and replied 'that is my luggage, I can take care of that' in a rude voice. 'Why are you being rude, I will drop you police station come with me'.

He walked away beside me, I was still stood and looking his back, he stopped and turned and said 'you like leaving opportunities' I make annoyed face then I rush towards the luggage and dragged that, I exit from the airport he was resting his back on the Honda city accord a purple car, to be frank I like Honda city and with the purple shade it look sexy.

He wear sunglasses to hide his swallowed eyes, he is very cool, I like boys who do hard work they look cool. I went nearer he asked 'do you know how to drive?' I replied 'yeah...but' before listening my reason he threw the car key and I catch that but I was thinking how he can trust someone in minutes. He sit on the passenger seat and i sat on the driving seat, In a minute before I was plugging the key he turned his face towards the window and fall sleep, I was thinking he is that much tired!, then he said peacefully with sleeping voice 'go straight turn left , straight then left then continue with straight you will find police station' I smiled for his cleverness, I start the engine softly, I drive very rarely but my driving is very soft my colleague feel better even my mama 'aww' I am missing them very much, I am sure she was lying on a sofa and thinking about me that why I did not call her yet.

I was whispering with myself that how I will manage everything, it is very difficult to survive with money then I thought I will borrow some money from police officer and if he refuses. I thought, I will ask from him but he is tired he can definitely refuse me. Today, I get to know the most significant thing the earth is 'money and phone' but both I don't have. I looked at him, he was in a deep sleep it is looking that it is true he did not sleep for nights that is the reason his eyes swollen, his closing eyes and his tanned face make glow, he look beautiful when he sleep. I drive for minutes, the car atmosphere is in peace, suddenly his phone buzzed, he was sleeping very deep that he cannot able to heard so, I picked the phone with left hand switching the phone into silent mode.

We reached on the police station; it was not that far, I stop the engine softly. I wake him up with silent voice. He opens his half eye with rubbing his left eye and groggy from sleep, he asked me with taking yawn 'are we reached'

'Yeah..Are you coming inside too?'

He gives me his strong smile and said looking in my eyes 'no, I am very tired, I had to go home'

I smiled with raising my eyebrow and said 'by the way, it is okay for you drive in tiredness'

'Yeah…it is become my habit now and... .' hold sometime and said 'you're driving is very soft, I fall in deep sleep' ‘yeah…I know’ I opened the door while looking at him ‘so take care and sweet dream and also thank you for leaving me here’ I stepped out from the car while he also steeped out, while I was moving, he said with resting his left arm on the roof ‘thank you to make me sleep for minutes’ then I remembered that his phone was buzzing so I said ‘by the way, someone was calling maybe she is your girlfriend’ I laugh looking at him and move towards the police station. I did not see behind but he sat on the driving seat and start the engine roughly the voice was enough.

I entered on the police station they all were taking snacks and tea, the criminal were shouting some are threaten the police officer and some are guilty for their crime. The police officers were all free they have nothing to do, so one of the benches was empty so, I sit down. One of the police officer came to me with rubbing his finger inside the nose he said with splitting the ‘tambkoo’ ‘kya hua madam, kuch chori ho gya kya’ everybody laugh at his shitty joke but I don’t understand how he get to know, again one of the low post police officer stand beside him and said 'yeh toh north side ki lgti hein pkaa bag chori hua hai' again everybody laugh on their joke they both give high five to each other, suddenly the telephone buzzed 'tambkoo officer' picked up the phone and talking 'ji sahib ji sahib' and when he drop the phone he whispered something to another police officer than he come near me and say 'give some water to mam, order samosa for mam' what is that some sudden change occur , he make me sit to other bench and ask me about everything happened, he do some formalities to register in F.I.R. He give me samosa and the bottle of Bisleri, I was very thirsty and starving so, I did not refuse to take that. It taken hour and hour to sitting on police station they were working hard to find the suspect many thief's they find but not the one who stolen my bag.

I was sitting on the bench my hands were trembling about how I will do such things; I do not have that much strength to call my mama so I drop that plan many times in my mind. I heard of snoring so, I raised my back to look but that was a suspect who was sleeping in a jail, his snore disturbing people, he remind me of tired guy, I get back my strength because of him, but he also leave me, I had to borrow the money for him, I was scared what if he refused me to give money, then my ego will be hurt, telephone buzzed again the nearby police officer picked up the phone again after saying 'ji sahib and ji sahib' he give a symbol to another lady officer she came near me and said 'madam, let's go'

I replied with my watery eyes 'I cannot sleep for a night; I don't have nowhere to go'

She said with keeping my hand on my shoulder 'don't worry, the safari Jypsee will take you some place' I was thinking a safari jypsee is some sort of a magical car if you will ask to drop America the car will drop you, such a liar officer. Anyways, I don't know where to go so, I trust the magical safari.

When we get exit from police station, the night was there may be 7 or 8 pm was happening. I sit on the magical safari, it was damn good man! the lady officer ask the driver to drop me in Red diary café, I was thinking why they were sending me in some sort of café the name was pretty good 'red diary' I impressed. Back to the magical safari, the lady officer also came and sit in front of my seat, she was very silent and arrogant, the safari and the lady officer in front of me I was feeling myself a criminal.

I take a nap in magical safari, the lady officer wake me up with expressionless face, it seems like half n hour waste for dropping me in red diary cafe, I was thinking why they drop me in some café even there were not hotel anywhere, maybe they kidnapped me, i came out from the safari, the lady officer put the hand again on my shoulder and said 'go inside', you are very safe now'. I turned my head back, it was a beautifully design red café, whole walls very paint with esthetic red colour, the symbol of the café was 'it was open red diary inside it was written red diary café in calligraphy font'. The café was beautifully designed; every person who is walking was looking at the café. Anyways, may be the café owners part time job is giving shelter to poor people. So, I entered with dragging my suitcase, I pull the glass door even from inside the café was beautiful, the table chairs was red too, even the counter was red. I looked over the owner, he was looking like a Korean man fair and soft skin with short eyes and sharp nose and fully pink lips. He looked at me because of the voice of shutting door, I raised my eyebrow, he rush toward me and hug me and said 'thank god, you came here safely, if you were late for more minutes, someone had killed me' he was a chilled man and kind of funny, he was behaving like I know him from many years but then I thought who the hell is person that care for me in the Kolkata, I don't know anyone in the Kolkata, I asked him fluently 'who will kill you', he said with giving happy expression 'it is surprise for you, young lady' his body acting like he is gay. Holy shit! I was thinking he is very cute; I can date him but his posture saying he is gay.

He make me sit and asked me ‘if I had to order something very expensive, I can’ but I tell him to give me a water bottle and the noodles, he give me a great smile, actually he is amazing person if he was not a gay, I will definitely date him. I was bit confused that who is that great person, who is helping me if it is mom, yash, naina maybe akash not at all, how this guys will help me, maybe the tired guy, not at all he was very tired, he is sleeping right now, how he can help a strange person.

He came with noodles in his right hand and the bottle of bisleri in his left hand and said ‘my noodles are very delicious, you will love that’, I said looking at the dish ‘hmm…let’s see’, he take the front seat and sat,I taste that and it was really delicious, I looked at him ‘ummmm…it’s very delicious even, your café is delicious’ he laughed and I laughed too and suddenly he pick a chit from his pocket and give me with white envelope, ‘the surprise is that..’ hold and keep his finger on envelope ‘I am going now' add that. He stands and walks away, I looked at him walking away, I looked at the chit and envelope with quiet nervous face, and I took the chit and read, it was written

I am that tired guy, '9897666555' don't call me right now

I am in a deep sleep 4000 rupees amount is in the

Envelope maybe that is enough for you

Pay me back at tomorrow 10am

At this café

That chit increase my heart beat even my body was paralyzed, I cannot feel my internal organ, they were all stop working, that crazy bastard help me even in his sleep. awwwwww! He is damn cool, I should go on a date with him but he already have a girlfriend. That is very unfair, but why he helped even he was very tired, whatever it is but he is damn cool. I eat noodles with my smile, I was happy every second I was reading the chit. I was shouting on the café 'awwwwwwwwwwwwwwwwwwwwwwwwwwww' at every minute the people and that Korean gay man also looking at me with weird face, may be they were finding me weird. After eating my noodles, I walk to the Korean man

'Thank you for giving me food, can you tell me, where is low cost hotel nearby'

'Behind my café, there is guest room, you can sleep there'

'by the way, what is your name'

'Vivek thapa' he hold and give his card and say 'if you need any help call me and sweet dreams' I smiled him and went off from the café with dragging my suitcase. I find the guest room, it was my luck there is one room left, they give me key, I give them advance and move to my room. The room was very short but I was very tired, I ignore the room structure and lay down on the bed, my ribs and my back was hurting so much. I was very tired, i was dirty too. So I went to the bathroom to take a shower. I came out from bathroom and open my suitcase for my flip flops and night suit, while I was taking out my night suit, I found a black plastic bag, I take out and open , the money was there maybe it was 30000 rupees that my mama was giving to and I refuses. when I count the rupees it was exact 30000, I was get annoyed that why I did not look at my suitcase, I don't had to go to police station and that red diary café, but just then I see a that chit on the table.

I pick that chit and lay down on my bed and whispered 'if I opened my suitcase, I will never meet this tired guy'

I read the chit million of times in that night, I don't know why I was reading the chit millions time but still the chit was giving me relax, maybe I fall for him in night , I don't remember, when I fall sleep that night.

When I wake up, I look on the clock, it was 11am, I step out from bed with shouting 'noooooooo' It was very late, if he left. I quickly rush towards the washroom take shower and wear my new clothes, accessories and perfect fragrant deodorant. My stomach was bit paining, it was the butterflies in my stomach, I left my room and rush toward the café, I was wishing 'please god, make him stuck in the café'. I reached toward the café, I pull the door, he turned, he was there standing on the counter, he looked more handsome than from the other day, he comb his hair even his eyes was looking fresh, he cleaned his amazing beard, older day he was amazing but today he was looking perfect.

He looked at me with smile; his face was looking like he was waiting for me and now his wait is over. I stop to make the gaze, my stomach was paining now more, he was just seven steps away from, I take all my steps very slowly to look into his for long time, I was just one step far from him but still he was looking at me with his attractive smile and he muttered with clearing his throat 'hii'

'hello' with raising my hand I said 'I am saira rajput' he smiled and he shook his soft, gentle hand in my palms, his fingers were very gentle and he said 'Mihir banerjee; nice to meet you saira', I was thinking to be fall on the ground, my name was become more beautiful with his voice. I rubbed my neck with nervousness and said 'did you sleep well'.

'after, leaving you, I was bothering, if you will be okay or not, so, I call police officer , after going back to home, you were still on my mind so, after hour I called again to police officer to drop her in red diary café, then I came here with chit and envelope and asked him to help you; then I sleep well and wake up at 10' what was that, he was bothering me, I was in his mind and I muttered 'so, you are a police officer too'.

He smile and look at Vivek and said 'I am a detective', I put my both hand on my mouth and said 'whoa! Like Sherlock Holmes'; he chuckle on my nonsense talk, to be frank when he laugh or smile he look more attractive even his profession is attractive too, how can someone not fall for him.

‘But what, you tell to police officer’ his take one step close and whispered on my ear ‘I will tell you later’.

I take out his money and give him as it is and he said ‘you did not use this’

‘When I open my suitcase, I find money in my bag that my mom keeps it silently; I am very sorry, I bother you’

‘no, it is all okay’

‘so, now I had to leave right’, I turned back without listening his voice, I was hoping that he will stop me and asked me for date but I thought so much maybe he will stop me then the voice came loud enough form to hear over ‘hey..you look beautiful when you drive’ what was that, did he said I am beautiful, yeah I am, then I step back and look at him and said ‘but you were sleeping ,right’ he muttered ‘sometimes’. I smiled with glittery eyes, I was wondering that what will replied him so, I decided to leave and just then I thought, I again turned back and said ‘can you help me to explore this city’ I don’t where I got that courage to ask him but still, I glad he will say yes and he came closer to me hold my hand and said 'let's go' I was smiling from behind.

We came out from the café, I asked him about his car but he said he drive his car only for office.

'Do you eat breakfast' with caring expression

'I forgot to take breakfast'

'let's go to flurys breakfast'

We took yellow taxis, we both sit on the taxi, while on the route, we were talking about likes and dislikes, I was telling him about my yesterday heavy day and he was telling about his working hours. He is very talkative maybe he has no one else to talk about his lives; I want to know about him everything, every single thing from his routine to his past. He doesn't know, he look more beautiful when he talks as I completely fall for him.

We reached on Flury's breakfast, it is look like a café, and its walls are paint with pink and blue color. Everything, was seems perfect in that café. We sat on the chair, he calls one of the waiter, he ordered some deserts and sandwich. He gives me smile and I can only smile back then he makes him comfortable with his chair it is looking more like a date.

'Do you know, why I came to Kolkata' I started the conversation

'Yeah…for being cool' I laughed and said 'yeah…that is my second reason; next'

'You love Kolkata'

'Yeah…that is the third reason; next' with raising my three fingers

'Maybe…you want to meet me'

'Yeah…that is perfect reason' we both chuckle on this non-joke.

'Because that is my dream from 18 that I will celebrate my 25th birthday in Kolkata'

'About Kolkata, you have to dream for America, Italy or Greece somewhere; you are not cool anymore'

‘Why, do you think Kolkata is boring?’

‘But it is not coolest place also’

‘I don’t want to be a cool; I just want to start my trip from Kolkata’ our ordered came, the deserts were beautifully designed. I ate and he said ‘so, it is your birthday today’

‘Not today, but tomorrow’

‘Whoa’ his expressing seeming like, he does not have any interest in my birthday, that is very bad of him, I tell him and he ignored my thing very easily.

We came out from the flurry’s breakfast after having a wrangling that who will pay the bills it was him who won. I was standing on the exit door, suddenly the rain drop fall, after paying the bill he came outside and I asked him to walk till the Hooghly River, it was far but still it was okay to walk in the cloudy weather. We walk for few miles and suddenly the rain started, I look upwards to the sky and he hold my wrist and make me rush towards the tramp ride, we both climb on the ride, my hand was resting in his chest and he holding my left elbow from his right hand, and from his left hand, he was rubbing his head as his head was wet, after a few seconds, we realized that we were very close, we take step back. Awkwardness was refining in our faces, we both were losing our gazing.

Back seat was vacant, so I sat on the seat. My next was vacant too, he also sat on that and then again our elbow touches, it was again an awkward scene but for ignoring, I start a conversation 'it is still raining, right'

'Yeah…I can see'

'So, where this ride stop'

'maybe nearby howarah bridge'

'ohoo, so our sunset is not miss'

'Yup'

Our awkwardness was still not left; we were again losing our eye contact. The moment when we were very close, is the best moment of the day, his eyes look more beautiful from near, and even his perfume fragrance was bless my nose.

I looked at him with raising my eyebrow, he smiled, I can only give him back my smile. My long hair was flying everywhere, even it was touching his eyes maybe he was getting irritate. He said with leaving my hair on his eyes 'maybe, you have to tie your hair'

'Yeah… I am very sorry'

I open my tiny bag and take out the rubber band, while I was tying my hair, my head burst on the window 'ouch' with touching my head, he was looking on the other side, my voice make him look into my side.

'Can I' with caring tone, I slowly give my rubber band to him. He softly holds my hair with his soft gentle hand and ties my hair. 'Thank you'

He give smiled and I said with looking into his eyes 'today, you don't had to go for work'

'I take two day off for my hard work'

‘Okay’

‘When you will be depart from Kolkata’

‘My plan was to stay for week but I have less money and no phone, so I decide to depart after four days’

‘Yeah… four days are enough to visit’

We reached on the Howarah bridge to see a sunset in hoogly river, we were not so far from the pincep ghat. We both walk over the bridge, he share his school story that how, they were desperate to bunk the class of his ‘mukeshpanwala’ teacher and run toward this bridge to drink ‘chikange’. He asked me to share one of my school stories, but I was a boring front bench girl who is struck with family problems like the fight of my mother and father.

We reached to our destination talking about our families and profession, about his family he does not have any siblings, he lives alone in the flat near his office and mother father leaves in another house that is far from his flat, he meet them in weekends. His profession was not easy to understand, he work in the private detective company, eventually his office is like Brooklyn nine nine difference is that his company is private, sometimes it took night and days to watch a security footage, even though they know, they cannot find anything but for a clue, they had to work. In Brooklyn nine nine their work was easy and funny but in reality it was bit opposite even he hates his team and colleagues but he love his profession so much.

After knowing everything about ourselves, it was time to travel in boat for looking the sunset closely. We put the jackets; he gave me hand to climb in boat [that was cool] we both stand on the boat, I was bit trembling but then after some seconds it was fine, the howrah bridge and the falling down sun was perfect; lying on the boat between the river and the voice of flowing water makes my skin shiny, makes my body soft and flying of hair with slow falling down sun, squeezing the clouds over the sun, it was all shining in my eyes my pupil turn into yellowish black, if we turn back it was all being dark. It was looking like our boat moving in the shine and behind our back was all dark, like we are coming from a dark to see the shine in the eyes. We both looking on the sun and hearing the sound of flowing water, he lay down on the boat, I lay down to beside him, his perfume was bit like a jasmine flower and maybe lavender. He was so nearer to me, I turned towards him, he turn with me too, our face were just 10 mm away, her eyes was looking more beautiful nearer, looking into his eyes, It was like the whole universe stop and my body paralyzed too. His nose was looking more straight, I can now very well recognize his perfume even he will be one meter away from me, I was wishing from inside maybe this moment stop for a while, the bright falling down sun squeezing of clouds over, this cannot for a while?; I cannot whisper in his ears, that I fall for him?; cannot I kiss him? That was question on my veins and vessels.

After looking at each other for while, he was the one destroy our gazing maybe he was uncomfortable or may be awkward. Our boating was end, it was a most admirable and gorgeous thing of Kolkata, the best part was when I look into his eyes.

After traveling some mile with taxi and walking, he asked if I am non vegetarian or not and I tell him that of course I love eating non-veg, if you never eat chicken in your entire life then probably, I shall skip talking to you. He took me to the best shop of roles in Kolkata 'Kusum rolls' his uncomfortable and awarkwardness was left when we reach to Kusum rolls because he was in joy, probably he loves rolls. He was exploring me Kolkata for joy and I was exploring because of his adorable smile. He asked me to play a game with menu sticking on the wall of that shop, he asked me to close his eyes and he will start with numbers and I had to stop him in any number and whatever roll it is written on the number , I shall had to eat that even though, I does not like roll. The game was very cool, so

I closed the eyes for his sake, he started saying numbers and I stop him in number eleven as it is my birthday number, I got chicken roll [woah; my lucky number work]. When the roll was cooking, it was his turn, I started saying number and he stop me in twelve and it was vegetable roll. The vegetable role make me laugh very bad, his face was very dull because he want to eat some chicken stuff roll and it was not his luck. My laugh was not ending and that make him annoy, it was my very well turn to tease and I do that.

We got our rolls, when I take the bite of chicken roll 'yummmmmmm' with teasing manner, his face was still in dull but still he take a bite of his roll 'it is also taste well, you should taste that' I taste the bite, it was probably good but not more than chicken, I make him taste my roll too. In one bite he eat the half of my roll, that makes me annoy and I slap him on his shoulder and still he was laughing to tease me. One roll was not sufficient for us so, we both take again chicken roll.

Our night had an end after taking the rolls, we eat ice cream. I have some sufficient money, so I change my hotel, probably he helped for shifting and we both walk away each other but then he shout my name from behind 'saira, it is your birthday right, meet me again in Red diary café at 9 or 8 morning and good night' I just smile at him and shake my head, I shout and said 'ok'. I walk over my room without looking at him, maybe he walks away. I was very tired, so I dressed up and lay down on my bed thinking about every great moment we shared softly. when I fall sleep, I never know and then at midnight my phone buzzed, I picked up my phone, It was vivek he tell me with gasping that Mihir got in a accident and he is standing front of my hotel.

I did not even thought about my clothes I wore take my flip flops and rush down stair without looking everywhere, vivek was standing on reception in care tone, I asked 'is he is okay, take me to him', he hold my hand

and make me walk away from the hotel, he start his engine, I sat on the car and he make me smell chloroform and when I went unconscious, I never get to know, probably from my experience it was very dangerous.

When I wake up, I was in the backseat of vivek car maybe, I was very angry, I step out from the car, I was standing front of Red diary café, I went inside. The light went off and someone was doing countdown murmuring 1,2,3,4,5,6,7,8,9,10 and then the lights went on and all together ' happy birthday' it was them Mihir, vivek and the red diary chef and one waiter, I was smiling that it was very well surprise, I was in the shock that even my best friends never do this things to in my entire life, my hair, dress, looks ,were so clumsy but the happiness in my eyes and face realizing me the brighter from all of the people standing near my side.

They came out from the kitchen with cake and the blowing candle, I cut my birthday, I give a thanks hug to each of them, the Mihir was standing at the last holding his arms together with his lovely smile, I came closer and hug him without any hesitation, he whispered in my ears 'bengali loves do such stuff'. His words make me chuckle, I was happy to listen that, it was one of the Mihir plan and he is the one who take the help from peoples to make my twenty fifth birthday a little interesting. He walked with me to the hotel, it was not so far but still each moment with him is like the time running ten times faster.

We reached to the hotel, I was waving him and he said 'did you ever been in a relationship'

'I tell you right, I was always been stuck in family problems of my father in high school and after college I never got anyone or maybe I was in my own zone that is the reason, I never felt of romance'

Beside the hotel, there was a house with four stairs, he sit down on the stairs and asked me to sit beside with him, he point the finger on the stars and the moon

‘Do you ever look at the moon in the dark midnight’

‘Sometimes’

‘probably not in Kolkata’

‘Do you know the difference between of midnight moon and the night moon’

‘Maybe not’

‘in evening or night our ears were on loud and we can never focus on this beauty and in midnight our ears were on peace it help us to focus on the moon even the backside it was all dark’

‘Are you a selenophile?’

‘not in the night but in midnight’ I chuckle, he looks at me with his beautiful eyes

‘Do you never have a girlfriend before?’

‘yeah…one in my office, she was too beautiful when I look at her, I was a confident man so, one day I tell her that I like her and she agreed to that because in office everybody respects for my hard work, I was in everybody eyes, it was a bless two weeks and then I get to know about her hate and rude and sometimes a psycho behavior and the time comes where my attraction is end and I realized, I never loved her so, probably there is no women I fall in love'

'whao! I thought you love story will be awesome but it is not'

He chuckles and said 'you were so boring in your high school but I want to know about your mom and dad story'

'so, may be you know that rajput are so powerful people or a violent right, but my nani was not violent but off course my nana was like 'I can conquer this universe' type person, and one day my mom fall in love with my dad in Delhi university ,when they first meet in class, that time my father was very innocent or a shy boy and a very loyal men and probably my mom have a genes of rajput so, she fall in love with his opposite genre man, then they decide to get married and my mother was the first to get approach for a marriage, he belongs from pandit that makes my nana a bit upset, he always want a grandchild to be a powerful rajput and he was refusing for a marriage but then my smart nani makes a deal that we will give our daughter on one thing, if our grandchild never get changed the surname she or he will remain rajput and unfortunately, my father was orphan so, it was no big deal for him and he get agreed to that. Then I born with a surname of rajput, my eleven years was in very peace and then my father had to transfer in Agra and he meet a attractive women, she was nice but the bad thing is that my father cheats my mom and when I reached in my high school it was all war and sadness in my house and he decided to get married then my mama probably had to leave him, it was all sickness in our minds and our nana was also died on that fucking upset year and we moved to my nana nani house for sake of my nani, it takes times to change everything but then in my college life, we were finally get adjust, my mother become a headmaster of the school and my father leave that women and married to other one. If we talk about now, he is doing affair and cheating his current wife'

'I am sorry, your high school was probably a destroy year'

'It is okay, now all the thing does not bother me'

'Do you talk to your father?'

'Yeah…. Sometimes because my mother said look at him as a father, he will look good don't look at him as my husband, he will look devil; he love me, he care for me, on summer vacation I live with him with my step mother and brother they were too good; every weekend she came to my mom school for apologize and they become best friends now'

'I am sorry but if I were you, I will never talk to my dad'

'Yeah….but every day you cannot ignore someone efforts; my dad loves me even my mom too but his demon inside making him do such things'

‘You live a life very softly right, even devil looks beautiful in your eyes’

‘You live a life very roughly, even the beautiful people look devil in your eyes’ staring at each other for a minute, he is one who destroy our gaze.

‘Maybe, I should leave’

‘Well…Good night then’

‘Happy birthday, once again’

He walks away and I went inside in my hotel room. I was very tired and I lay down at the bed, there were many thoughts arrived in my mind ‘why he give me a beautiful surprise’, ‘did he fall in love with me’ or ‘he was saying right that, Bengali people do such things’, ‘so why then he ask about my relationship status’ and ‘why he talk to me for such long’, ‘why he was the one make a surprise for me’, ‘why he agree in a second for exploring the city’, ‘why he was the one, who help me even in his sleep’, ‘all the question have one answer “he fall in love with me”, ‘I should ask him’ or ‘I should wait for his first move'. At the end I decided that, I should wait for his first move. When I fall sleep and when my eyes open after many hours, I never get to know.

Today, is the most excited birthday of my life, 'it's my birthday today' all my internal organs shouting from inside, I pick up the best dress of my collection and the gladiator boots shoes with a little make up on my face to look brighter but I was stuck with my hairstyle, if I open my hairs, my hair look thick and rough and again that will irritate Mihir, if I do pony tail my hair look thin, so at the end I decided to do a messy braid and it actually work. I was looking damn perfect and I lock my room and give keys in reception. After drawing every boy attention, I went off from the hotel, and Mihir was standing across the road with black shirt and the dark blue jeans and the oxford shoes, he was looking beautiful even in his black sunglasses. After looking at me, he waved at me; I came across to him 'you are looking beautiful today'

'Even you look handsome too'

'Every weekend or my day off, I look like this only; there is no change'

'But there is change for me' I look at behind ant the parking area and said 'you still not come with your car; today weather is too hot'

'I hate driving; I just use my car in the office because to chase the criminal fast, I need of the damn car'

'Car is not a purpose for chasing, look at me, I am looking perfect now after an hour my sweating will make me ugly'

'I did not said we will not take taxi'

'What is the schedule?'

'Do you think, I am your personal assistant?'

'No…..'

'So believe in me and come with me, we had to chase the taxi'

'uffffff…man; you will chase that'

We take a yellow taxi and whole time, we were discussing about the advantage and disadvantage of cars, I was in a favor and he was against. Even the driver was irritate by our wrangling of this stupid talk, then we started talking about where he is taking me and why he is not telling me anything and then the time come where our taxi stop and we were standing on the gate of Victoria Memorial and the vivek and his waiter were standing with the two similar soccer bicycle, and then he tell me that with bicycle it is more fun than the chariot ride, I was very upset as I hate ridding bicycle and the men I am with, is a stubborn. Finally, we had to ride the bicycle after all with my upset mood. I look at the chariot ride, he knows very well that I want to sat on that but because of him, I am using this bicycle and he stop and come beside me and tell me that when he was a kid, his mother used to take him in the morning with his bicycle and she walk, he ways insist him to take the chariot ride and once he sit on that chariot ride, it was probably slow and he was getting bored, he likes it but not more than a bicycle, he also says me that 'the thing which you ride by yourself is very different than you used to sit on that and admire the things' He tell let's do a race of admiring every beauty of this Victoria memorial.

I ride a bicycle speedy, his speed was more than me sometime we came to each other and sometimes he came first and I become the last, our laughing was unstoppable, I share my lame jokes and he act like he did not like that, he was really right riding a bicycle is more fun than sitting and just admire and admire. If we sit on that damn chariot ride, our competition and laugh will be get in loss. We stop on the ice cream parlor and we take our favorite ones and co incidentally our favorite ice cream was 'flingo'. We eat that ice cream and talking about which ice cream flavor is best or worst. Our Victoria memorial had an end.

It is the time to go the Gariahat with tram ride, it is one of the best traditional market of all time, Bengali sarees were the most famous in there, we climb on the tramp ride, eventually it was no space to sit, so we choose to stand and the best thing it was that one of the couple had taking over the seat and they were covering their face maybe they were kissing. We both together look at them and look at each other and I don't know why we laugh with silent, it was no conversation Nothing but still it was looking very creepy everybody look at us with weird face, their face make us laugh again silently, still there was no conversation, I was giving him the symbol to don't laugh and the ride stop with jerked, and the couples both remove their jackets. Holy crap! They were lesbian and that make us laugh again but this time we laugh loudly with hiding our faces. They all again look at us with weird face even the couple get to know that we our making fun of them.

Our tram ride had stop and we climb off from tram ride, the Gariahat was just one kilometer away so, probably we had to walk again. About not talking in the tram ride and laughing loudly, we were discussing about all the things even the couples that we find were lesbian and old man who is acting to reading the newspaper and looking on the couples with judgmental eyes. When we reached to Gariahat, we also not know, he tell me that in this market you have to know the bargaining skills and eventually we don't had to buy anything, I just want to buy five traditional bengali saree for naina, ria, mama, nani and me. The market was fully crowded, he tell that there is the shop of his friend of Bengali saree and we will get the best discount from them. We reached to that showroom with pushing everybody who cane nearer to our, the showroom was little bit large. He make me wore a worst and cheap saree and when I look at mirror, I was looking a maid, the sales girl was finding us very weird but in fun we lose our manner for time.

Finally, we take the saree, he take for his mother too and probably I choose for my (mother-in-law), he also tell me that his mother have a very interest in saree wherever she goes for travel, anywhere she go she come with a saree too, when she go to Indonesia, she took the best and expensive saree from there.

We walk over every place and did not buy anything; we both were showing our bargaining skills here and there. I take one hand made diary, even though I know, I will not use them.It was being afternoon something 4:00 pm and we were starving like hell and the weather was hot as hell, so we took the yellow taxi for Indian coffee house. It took many minutes to find one taxi, I was killed from inside and when we both sit inside the taxi and the driver turn on the A.C, it was feeling like after having much Torture in hell, we got a heaven.

I never know when my head fall on his shoulder and his head on my head. When we fall sleep, we don't know after it happened sunset, we both wake up and we reached to the Indian coffee house. We were just blank it was like we are waking after years and whatever it happened we don't know anything, the driver tell us that 'we stuck in a heavy traffic jam for an hour and you both guys are sleeping like you both were very tired, so I didn't wake you up and one thing you both look perfect with each other'. The driver was very good he give more money because he deserves to be get as he said we were looking perfect.

The Indian coffee house was between the book market, we walk many miles again, I asked him every second 'where is coffee house'. And finally we reached there, we walk upstairs and it was like a old café of 90's with big hall and the old huge fans hanging on wall a very crowded place. It feels like I came at the time of independence, Mihir tell me that if you take one coffee, you can sit many hour also; you can read your book or write a book anything. We both ordered the two coffee and fish curry.

'Your office is tomorrow right' I started the conversation

'Yeah…don't make me sad please'

'Why?'

'My days with you were outstanding, you cannot even imagine and now again criminal records, suspect, footage and blood, I am get used for this'

'In 25, I have never enjoy my birthday like this; I used to hate my birthday, where people are excited for their Birthdays, I pray to god that my birthday will never come because at the end I shed my tears'

'heh…. It's okay, such things happen just for good, maybe god want you to love your 25 birthday' (I Chuckled) and our order came, with our starving stomach, we did not see here and there and focus on our food, it was a bit funny and weird but you will never understand the starvation from morning to the evening. After filling our empty stomach, our legs were paining so we decide to sit here for bit and then we will be roam around the market. We talk about everything, he started telling that he miss his school friends so much and now he is very lonely with no such friends, everyone is busy with their career and family.

After talking about bad thing about our school, we roam in book market, I take some books and I tell him that my favourite novel is 'Trevor Noah- Born a crime'. The novel is the best, the character of the mother and the author was too strong and funny. That novel makes me cry and make me laugh too. So, that's why it is the best and I did not read many but some recommended novels I read. Into this he does not like reading and writing, when he was a kid his father bring detective comics and he fall in love with detective lives and fall in love with criminal and investigation.

We take a yellow taxi for to reached in red diary café, entering in the red diary café with very tired it is like, you are laying down in the garden with many flowers around you, blowing your mood, his waiter were working and he was in standing in the counter, making a money slip for customers, 'broo, how was your day' vivek said

'very tired man, bring up two noodles'

‘heh… ashish take their order’.

I take French fries and the noodles, vivek came and sit with us with stress face, sit beside Mihir and say ‘man…customers are not coming the way they come older week, all my maintenance are in debt’

Mihir: how much money you want?, maybe I can give some

Vivek: thanks man, but I don’t want to take more debt from you

Me: hey guys, customers are not coming, the problem is that right

Vivek: yeah…but saira maybe my food is not good enough

Mihir: do you have a plan for this

Me: I don’t have plan but people are attracted in this café by this beauty more than food, so why don’t we elaborate this more

Vivek : beauty?

Me: no dumb; now I have a plan

Mihir and vivek : what? [all together]

Me: day after tomorrow, we will come up with a one year ceremony and starting of karaoke competition

Vivek: did you mean that, we had to celebrate one year ceremony with a damn karaoke competition.

Mihir: no dumb, she means that we will do one year ceremony and also we will start karaoke in your café from day after tomorrow

Vivek: woah!

Mihir: and the best thing is that there is no karaoke in our locality

Me: do you have that much money for ceremony and the karaoke

Mihir: I will invest on that; just give me 2% of your share

Me: woah! Now it is all right vivek

Vivek is a very dramatic man, his eyes become red and he hug both of us for our great plan, our order was their then we eat some noodles and after that again they all came up with the cake 'happy birthday, saira' written on that lovely cake that made by red diary café chef.

We came out from the café, while walking on the street, he said thank you for my great plan and I tell him that I am a masters in marketing degree. I ask about his friendship for vivek then he tell me that, he is the kind of man, if you do one thing for him, if it is expensive or cheap it does not matter, for giving his debt he can give you anything even his soul too. 'I help him with a case and when we both become friends, we never get to know', I also asked him about his gay behavior and I was right he is a gay but the best thing Mihir is so close to him but he did not like him, he like his chef at first meet.

When we both reached to my hotel, we never know as I said, when I with him the time works ten time faster. It was the same scene as yesterday, he left me and I stare at his back until his back become blur but then I realized, he did many things to me and I did not even say him a warm 'thank you'. Then I rush and hug him and whisper in his ear 'thanks for everything; you will be become busy again but can I call you at evening or may be in night', he smiled with me and said 'when you get your phone back'[I chuckled] 'with hotel telephone', 'saira, I will not be there in morning but I will definitely be there in night', 'it is okay', 'can you leave my right hand', 'yeahh… I am very sorry'. What? I hug him and it did not matter for him, he just say leave my hand not even he said it is okay, he did not even say anything. Now it is confirm, he did not love, it just my mind lie. He walks away beside me with his smile and the glittery eyes.

My head was like busted with a temper, I entered in my room and shut the door with jerked, I lay down on my bed with a embarrassed body, put my tiny bag and shoes aside, 'I screwed up, I suck everything', 'I did not had to hug him', 'I should control my feelings'. After some time with thinking about all that in my mind, which I had screwed very much, but still talking with him is not always enough, being with him every moment was not enough, seeing him every time very closely was not enough, tomorrow I will not see him from morning to night, not see him breath, I cannot tell him properly that I like him, I cannot say to him that I want to talk with you more, cannot stare at him continuously with no voice, I never wish to be with him as her girlfriend or a wife, just want to know about everything in his life, every sadness, every happiness even though it is dangerous for me. His talkative eyes make me feel like; it is for such a minutes or days.

I wake up in the morning, with not so excitement, it was like I wake up at my rajput mansion with the same day, I did not even have a phone that I can call him, but I have the hotel telephone and 'what I will ask him?', looking at the window, I was thinking what he was doing right now?, is he is okay and then I had a thought that , if he cannot meet to me but I can meet him by visit at his office for just a exploration. So, I call him and he answer the call with saying ‘who’

‘it is me, saira’

‘hey saira, good morning, are you good? Anything you want’ in one breathe

‘I called you because; I want to visit at your office’

‘Well…yeah you can come but if it is okay for you to come alone here’

‘Yeah….definitely, I will be fine’

‘Okay…then I am telling you the address’

He tell me the address and I write that in one paper, with excitement I open my suitcase and take out my dress and go for a shower after being ready after some minutes, I locked my room and give the key to reception and take a taxi.

I reached there after some many minutes, it was a huge old building, he was standing on the gate and looking at his watch maybe he was waiting for me, I came to him, he smiled at me with saying ‘what take you so long’ and I replied with smile ‘your office is very far from hotel’, he was telling me about his team office is on upper floor, we take a elevator and we reached to his office all were shouting very ‘ohoooo’ and I was making a shy stranger face, he was smiling too and telling about some detectives like him who work very hard and some were actually looking like they were not sleep from decades. His office is whole look like a Brooklyn nine nine family, and there she was, using keypad very fast and his legs were in desk all were happy to see me but she was the only one with pink highlights on her hair and eating chewing gum, she was beautiful but he is correct his posture and everything is looking she is a very psycho and rude too. When I was meeting with people who he introducing to me and telling about their warm nature, she look at me with a killer eyes and walk towards to me, where I was looking at mihir with scared eyes, his face become pale to when she come closer to me and said ‘hey…mihir don’t you introduce her with me’, his face was pale yet too but very confidently he introduce me, I smiled at her but she smiled very rudely 'so you are his friend', 'yeah' I said murmuring, 'I am going to eat something; why don't you join me'. listening this words, I don't know what strange in her words but he hold my hand and came closer to her and say rudely 'no…she has a plan' she chuckle and I was looking at him with nervousness in my eyes 'I am not taking her to kill, it is just about five minutes, we will talk and she will go back', 'I said you n, she have a plans to do' with yelling, everybody stand out from their seats and watching the war with seriousness, she yell at him saying 'hey…don't mad at me' and it is my time to say something, I left his hand and said 'it is okay mihir…it is just about five minutes, I will go with her'. Mihir look at me with caring eyes, maybe he was worrying about my going with this psycho.

We both leave but I was looking at him maybe he say anything not even a bye after I tell him, he was continuously staring at me with beg eyes, even he was waiting for me if I deny to go with her and talk to him for sometime but I also want to know more about this damn 'psychopath'. She take me to one of the best restaurant near by their office, she order some dishes but I was not hungry so, I deny to order something, she was not forcing me to order something, she was very rude and arrogant, she did not even know how to smile sweetly may be she thinks herself a 'savage girl', 'so tell me one by one, what you two had done every damn moment' with his rude and killing eyes

'Why would I tell you?' I tell with patient voice

'because, I am sure, mihir still love me and she cannot fall for a unconfident and damn boring girl'

'Wow! And I know him very well that he never repeat his mistakes and regrets' she chuckles and say with arrogant face 'exactly that is, I am trying to say'. Her posture is true, she is definitely very savage but after having a damn insult, what will i say next 'do you want to know right, what happen with me and him' very confidently, 'yup' his little words are also look like that he is insulting me. she put her legs on her desk and flip her hair towards backside and put his arms together, I tell about everything, every moment that we both spend, every good thing from the starting to the end, I thought she will be get jealous but she was yawning and saying 'after that', damn she was thinking me a 'good night, story teller' after telling everything she stand and said 'okay…I got it', she stand and get out of my sight in minutes without saying anything, pays a bill in a counter and get off from the restaurant.

I want to go to meet my stepbrother in hostel, so I leave the restaurant and take a yellow taxi to reach the hostel. I reached to the hostel and meet my stepbrother, he hugs me a tight hug because we met after a very long time, I asked about her mother is okay and he was get angry on me that , why did not I tell him about my trip so he can pick me from airport and I was telling him that my phone and the bag with the money is stolen. I asked him to tell my mother that I am okay and my phone is stolen that is why I cannot answer her call. I meet his friends and see his hostel room and we talk about many things even our childhood memories, when I came to my dad house for stay. He takes a photo with me so he can share in his story with a caption 'after very long time'. After talking for hour, it was very getting late for me so, I went to my hotel. When I reached to my hotel it was happening evening, and the mihir car was standing, so I thought maybe he is here, i look everywhere in hotel but he was not there, then I thought maybe was sitting in that house stairs, so I rush towards there and he was sitting looking at the moon and I was looking at him, his side face look more beautiful eventually he was very far for me but even his blur face looking beautiful, for many seconds, I continuous watching him but then one old lady yell at me for being aside and his gazing eyes with moon destroy and look at me and he give me a smile and I smile him back, I rush towards him and

I want to tell him everything, every moment without him is hilarious, I want to tell him.

I sit beside him and asked him ‘how was your day?’, he give me a tensed look and said ‘sairaa’ for holding for a minute and stare at me he said ‘can I stare at your eyes for minutes and hold your hand for minute’, ‘is everything okay, mihir’, ‘you will be go away for me day after tomorrow right!’, ‘yeah but can you tell me what happened’, ‘saira…you will never come back right!, you will never makes me laugh again and again I will be alone for years’ my mouth was trying to say, if you will say to be with you for years, I will definitely stay with you but actually I said ‘hey…look at me, is everything is okay’. ‘yeah…but when I walk towards my office and home, I feel very alone saira’

‘Let’s go take me to your house’

‘Why?’

‘I come towards to your office and make a lovely memories and I will make again a lovely memories in your house too’

‘Do you know? I come with car’

‘I know and you will drive and I will sleep’ he chuckles and we both sit on car, we took seat belts and he said the car engine very roughly. I tell him about my stepbrother what we both do each other today, he was just giving me a smile and I was telling him a childhood memories with him, I tell him that when I stay at his home, we always feel awkward with each other at first, our friendship starts when his mom tell him to not go to play because of Delhi humidity, but he wants to play and one day his mom left with giving me a duty to watch him and he beg me too much, so I tell him he can go after than he had to come fast. Every time her mom left she tells me to do this duty and I let him go and one day he take me to meet his friends and where I met one girl and then we both go together he plays with his friends, I played and talked with mine and one day she caught us and that was the day was looking like a hell, she come closer to us but the best thing is that, she did not yell at me for not doing my duty but she yell at me because I was playing in the humidity, if anything happens to me, if I caught sick. Her scolding is not even fake, in her scolding it was care and love for another child. That time I get to know, the woman is not always evil but in love she pull herself in hell and become a evil woman.

In that meantime we reached to his home, and he tell me that in my story he taught that woman is not always evil but in love she pull herself in a evil woman. We reached to his apartment, his apartment was too short but for a single person, it is okay for survive. He make me sit on his short dinning and grab me a coke. He asked me about that psychopath and I tell him from the start, his eyes was looking like he is in a bit temper but then I asked about why he shout at her then he replied that he know very well about what he will ask to me and he was worrying if I bother about this things but the best thing, I did not bother about anything.

'you all look like a "Brooklyn nine nine family", but you are Amy Santiago who always want everything perfect and attention seeker of Boss' he chuckles while drinking coke and ask 'that is my favorite series, every weekend of midnight, I watch that series but wait a second why did not you say me Jake Peralta?' with pointing a finger on myself I said 'if I was in your office, I will definitely Jake Peralta, because I am chilled and cool in my office', with annoy face 'hey.. I don't like lies', 'no….i am saying true'. Then our wrangling started with matching our characters of movies and web series, unfortunately we both were against each other. Then after talking nonsense with each other, we decided to watch a movie 'kal ho na ho' as we both are in deep love with Sharukh khan acting and personality, unfortunately kal ho na ho is all time favorite. Our enthusiasm and sad was in the movie even though we know the ending, but still reaction in scene is must. After wasting three hours in movie, he left me in my hotel room with good bye and hug.

I wake up early in the morning and then I realized about today's ceremony of Red Diary café and i picked dresses for ceremony, It was all confusing, I was in the confuse for my red mini dress, basically for ceremony we decided the red code and one thing that making me sad is today is last of everything, my evening and night will be finished in the ceremony and I will not get time to talk to mihir and tomorrow morning I will be off, the feeling in my heart was very bad that everything will be finished like a rainbow we find in every rain and when it visible, it looks beautiful and we lost in the beauty that much that we cannot get to know, when it become invisible. That was going in that moment, but after all first I get to ready for today ceremony.

After having rest and doing lunch, I get a call from red diary café that i am the host of that ceremony, so I need a rehearsal for that, so I get ready very fast with my open long hairs and casual dress.

I take taxi for red diary café, it was evening and the temperature was hell like every day in

Kolkata. I entered on red diary café, everyone was busy in doing decorate the ceremony, even Vivek and the red diary café chef were busy in making some Bengali sweets [Bengali have a very good taste], i interfere the waiter, I asked him about my rehearsal, my hosting and all, unfortunately his answer was 'mam…there will be dance performance?', in my mind, I was thinking, how can Vivek hire some dummies they did not even know about, what is happening in the café, they are working, for not get anymore silly answer, I asked the Vivek for my hosting. In his head, it was pressure for ceremony but still he is a kind of person aside his stress and pressure and help people and talk nicely even though, he needs help. He welcome me with hugging and said that one of the best singer in the locality is going to sing a song for red diary café and I also convinced my chef to sing with blushing in his face, [I can read that well]. So, I take a corner seat in kitchen with paper and pen [actually, it was many tissue papers] without any further disturbance, I started writing my anchoring, apparently I am a good writer [you can judge me while reading my story]. I destroy many tissue paper with making hole in that. Finally when they all shout making ready every sweets and dishes, I also completed writing my anchoring, it was too hard so, the best moment was looking nobody around me, I dance with my own sign of happiness, it was weird for people who were in the kitchen but one of the waiter [the dummy one], he like my step, and he do again with me and the people around there also like my step, they also do with counting '1 2 3'. The moment was like 'attention seeker'. I was imaging Mihir on that people but that is not possible, it is many hour for him to come.

Until I came to terrace, the stage was ready just for rehearsal; lights were not still enough, I started doing my rehearsal, I added some beautiful words and sentence to attract the customers. When I was almost done for doing my rehearsal, the evening take a place, the lights were brightening perfect. In clock it was happening more than five, still there nothing about Mihir, the ceremony was about to begin, Vivek was calling him back to back but every time he was saying, I will be in ten minutes. The time comes when Vivek asked me to get ready for ceremony. In the mean time, I was almost forget about wearing a dress as I was busy in rehearsal and missing the Mihir from morning, the time went to come for meeting Mihir and suddenly they give me another task. I walk away for my hotel, to get ready after I sit on my taxi, he arrived with his car and stretching his head with looking turning his steering for parking lawn, I wish, I could say him 'HII', but if I do, he will definitely ignore.

After a bless hour, I was standing on hotel waiting for my cab to come but probably it is a 'fucking cab' [they need time, they cannot able to find my location even if I send my location]. Every story had is twist, like wise in my life, I am now a Cinderella, someone should come to take me and I will run out of that guy, so actually today I also have short love story with another guy.

As I said, I am a Cinderella someone should come and yup my hero is here [this time it is another guy]. I was standing waiting for my cab and one guy stop the car for me, he opened the window, I look at him [he is a average guy], his name is Prateek bhelsewala probably a marathi guy, he is one of the mihir colleague they are in same team, he recognized me very fast but I take some time. He approached me to sit on that car because he is going on same party, I did not said no to him, he came outside from the car and open a car door for me, I love the guys who have a best etiquettes.

He started a engine and I cancel the cab, it take 15 minutes to reach red diary café but he driving very slow it will take 20 minutes definitely actually the vibe coming from him is like, I am probably very safe, he started a conversation with smiling, 'mihir is a great guy and a funny guy', 'yeah..he is a type of guy who is very loyal for people' and he laugh like he is making fun of him 'not at all, he is the type of man who just use and throw people'.. I look at him with dangerous eyes 'how you can say this' he again laugh and said 'I am just joking..i know he is very loyal to people'. The thing I was thinking in my head before was coming opposite to the guy next me. Again he said with smile 'I always identify people with the phrase, I gave them in my head'..it was very interesting for me to know about my phrase and I asked him he said very softly looking at my eyes 'burn the ground at first meet' and i chuckle and said 'what for' and he chuckle, 'do you like that?'

Me: I like that but I need the reason

Prateek: the mihir screamed that psycho is for you, so you burn the ground and it is our first meet so what will be called?

Me: burn the ground at first meet

Prateek : exactly!

Me: and what is for mihir

Prateek: I have nothing for him but we called him a "angry pokemon"

Me: he is not a arrogant for his work he is maybe he not even cute like Pikachu

Prateek : you don't know anything about him, he is not chilled in office he is very angry with freshers and he told me that many girls DM him that you are cute like Pikachu your eyes were like Pikachu. The best thing he did not know his name.

I laugh and clap and said 'he really does not know about his know, you guys are so good'

I never get to know when we reached on the parking lawn when he stopped the car, I was chucking. He is a child guy, I don't like his first joke because, I talk to him very first and make him judge very fast although he is amazing guy, sometime I get bored with mihir but I does not get bored for a single minute with him.

We walk inside together and vivek give a sign with a finger for going upstairs. We went upstairs together and I saw him with black t shirt, he was looking adorable, he was talking with someone and suddenly, he look at me, he said 'hey' with enthusiasm, I thought, he is coming on my way but he hug him with saying 'mera veera agya' in Punjabi, and they both move with took hands on each other shoulders. I was probably ignored by him, he takes him to the group where they were sharing drinks and laughing, it was my bad insult. The temper in my head take me to the stage, to seek his attention, I take the mic.

I started giving my introduction with a soft jokes which people like to give smile on that and tell about my everything, how I met the vivek and mihir, people laugh on my stealing bag and the about criminal girlfriend but the best part is mihir was blushing and I said with more confidence 'give a clause one and only mihir banerjee for singing a song' his face was probably like 'what', 'what is happening' but he did not refused to come, everyone cheered him, I was clapping to cheer and he was climbing the stairs for stage and he came nearer and whisper in my ear 'what is your favorite song' and I said with smiling 'darasal', I thought he was joking but when I was getting down from stair he sit with his guitar and started the beat of darasal and I turned toward him and he look at me with a most sweetest and the lovely face, the face that I shall never be forget that face, it was that damn face and he started

“tum toh darsal khawb ki baat ho

Chalti meri khayalo mein sath ho

Milti hai jo achanak who sawgat ho”

I forget the people who were around me, it was just his voice which cherishing my ears, I don’t know he dedicating the song for me or not but the feeling and the vibes coming from his voice, is like he will never ever stop, he was looking at the guitar but I was looking at him with smile. My favorite song become 10 times more favorite and his voice stopped and the clapping started.

‘He gets down from the stage and it is the time came to call prateek on the stage, I just meet him 15 hours before’

He came to the stage and sit on the chair and took the guitar and I was getting excited that I can finally go to mihir and talk about many things but prateek hold my hand and asked me to sing with him for few lines in karaoke and without any excuse, I sit with him too, he was focusing on his song, singing 'Perfect song', I does not know the lyrics that much but he cover up the song with smartness, my intention was not to destroy his song but my brain just want to ran toward mihir but I can't, after some minute, it was time to invite some guest for karoke, I five my closing speech and ran towards the mihir everyone was trying the karoke and vivek and prateek were guiding them.

Finally he was alone waiting for me to come, I came to him, he asked me for the drink and I with a very shy manner, I agreed for drink.

Me: how I am looking

Silently prateek entered in our conversation and said 'not good this time', Mihir was drinking mojito and he chuckled, that makes me feel very insulted so, I walk away from their and started looking for my company but absolutely there is no one for me. Then Mihir came with by knocking my back and said 'you are looking fab, I think the word fab is made for you not the word even the dress, not even dress your hairs makeup beauty too'. After having many complains for him, he made me smile for the line that I did not even understand that what he said that but whatever it was very amazing.

In whole party, I tried not to stare him too much but when I stare him he give me smile too. We did not talk too much on that party because he seemed very busy with his colleagues, but at the very end when everyone was tried, he said, my speech and anchoring were best even I also said his voice and the singing was best.

While going back to our homes, he approached me to drop me hotel but I refused him because prateek already asked for that and I did not refused. On that party, our conversation being very formal. Prateek drop me hotel with striking many jokes in car but I did not enjoy his jokes that much because I was in the very off mood of going back meerut.

I lay down on my end like the ending story of my life, it was another stomach pain like somewhat aparting with people and independence. From starting it was very difficult to understand everything and manage the things but when mihir entered with his rough driving and the swalloen eyes was adorable.

I wake up in the morning and packing everything with grief and heavy heart, I check in my room and give keys and money in reception, I came out from hotel and waiting for Mihir to come and after waiting for ten minutes, he came with apologizing face. We both sat on the car, he told me that we will first go in the police station and asked about my bag, then the airport, on that car we were both silent, we both does not know what to say, not even discussing about second meet but just being silent and sorrow. We both reach on the police station , he asked me to go inside without him. I went inside without him and I asked about my bag their face were like ‘what is the meaning of bag?’, ‘who you are’, that makes me more feel sorrow. The lady without expression came to me and said ‘now everything is fine with your husband’, and everyone started laughing again and again I did not to know what they were trying to say. Then one of the man point the finger on mihir and said ‘aree dekho voh aya toh hei’ and I walk away with confused face.

Looking at my face, he get to know that I did not get my bag, while sitting on car, I said with making angry face ‘my 25000 is exploded even destroy too.’ He chuckled looking at me and said ‘you are so irresponsible’ and I said ‘please don’t make me angrier.

We both reached to the airport, helped me for the documents, and leave. In the childhood, the thing that I learned very great is that hiding the tears and he is the man, from birth they have a skills to hide tears. We were sad for the farewell that we never imagined of, but someday. I had to leave Kolkata, without looking at him, and stare into his eyes, I leave silently.

I was sitting on the window seat, I was very sorrow looking at window never know, when the air hostess make the announcement, never know when plane started to fly as my head was bursting with the memories of mihir and mine, all the laugh and the colours we have watch together, after some time, I started crying blindly, everyone was shocked while looking at me, they were very shocked and curious for my tears, sometime you cry because you feel very abandoned and lonely.

After many hours, I arrived in meerut, my mood was good because after many days, I will see my mama and comfortably take sleep on my bed.

When I entered in my locality, it was feeling like, I was not here for many years and days. When taxi stopped in front of my house, naina was in the balcony, she was doing oiling in my nani's head. When she look at me, she screamed with enthusiasm 'meri bhen agyi..meri bhen agyi', everyone in the colony was looking at me with honored eyes and I was just giving them smile and my nani expression was like 'kidar hei meri bittu, merko dikh kyu nhi rhi', I entered in my house to look over my mama with surprising entering, she was sitting on the sofa, I ran towards her and hug her but she was very angry, she refused to hug me and started beating me with 'chappal' and yelling at me ' I was calling you every minute and hour but you idiot never pick my call and after two days your stepbrother called me and said she is okay, her phone is robbed; then my heart beats properly after listening that you are okay', 'forgive me please, I will never do anything, please forgive me'.

After all she is mother, she hugged me and said 'what happened, tell me every single thing'. Naina and nani also came and said tell us also and I tell every single thing from stolen my bag to become friend with mihir.

They were happy and thankful for mihir [but they did not know that I fall for that guy too], but off course your best friend know everything and she get to know very perfectly that I fall for that guy.

I went to my room for some rest and after waking up for many hours, it was happening 8 pm and I was very hungry too so, I walk over to kitchen and I saw akash sitting with my mom and they were talking something very deep, I was in the mess dressed up and wearing shorts, I said 'hii' and he replied 'hey.. How was your trip', 'It was very good'. My mama was staring like, I will kill you, if you did not go inside, and I walk inside and lay down on the bed again, sometimes I thought my mom is having crush on akash., while making him my fiancé, she will marry.

I wake up in the morning with starving but this time, I walk out from my room with good clothes and now neighbor aunties were sitting and drinking tea with my mom and again same how was your trip and all that stuff. There are aunties and are not talking about my marriage, is not possible right, they were convincing my mom to talk akash family for marriage, [that is all bull shit]. that time, I realized, I don't have much time for mihir and he Is the person, who never agree to get married so early. Then I realize that I have to call her because to give him my new number.

I take naina for choosing the new phone; also we take SIM and other important things for phone. I came home and call him but he did not pick up my call but then I realized that maybe, he was busy with his work so, I did not disturb him.

In evening at 5 pm some what he called me with 'hello', and I said 'hey mihir, its saira from meerut'

MIHIR: hey how you are doing?

Saira: I am good; what is going on; how vivek café is doing

Mihir: I did not know so, we will get result very early, but I hope your plan will be damn successful

Saira: thanks for your appreciation

Mihir: is your mom is fine?

Saira : when I entered in home she beat me with 'chapal'

Mihir: she is so dangerous, man!

We both were chuckling on this topic after having very sweet talk, he end up talking with giving excuse, about his hungry.

I woke up early as weekend as over and I had to go for a office, my office holiday came to end. i ate breakfast with my family and walk away.

I reached in my office again the shocking reaction, again how was your trip and all that, what you have done? Why did not you pick up call on your birthday? And the same answer, my bag was being robbed, ria, yash and lucky were my real friends who I can assure that they will never judge me, so I tell them that, I fall in love with mihir, I thought that they will appreciate me or will happy for loving someone, but then they asked, did he loved you? And I said ‘I don’t know’ and then the drama started.

Ria: you should stop your feeling

Me : I can’t

Ria: do you know, he live very far from you, if he will fall in with you but also you will have a long distance relationship.

She holds and I said

Me: I will go and do a job their, that is not a matter

Yash: you have dream doing job in banglore; what are you doing with your life for that man, of whom you never know, will live with you forever or not.

Me: why are you guys, making things so complicated?

Lucky: hey, it is okay guys; you are putting all the things in his head

Ria: we are not putting things in her head, we are making her realized his practical life.

Me: ria, stopped it, I know you are possessive for me, missing him is more heartbreaking than any other thing

Ria: that's exactly, I am telling you, loving him that man, who is very far from is very heartbreaking; if you did not stopped your feeling now, your heart will break every time, whenever you will talk him.

Yash: I am with ria

Lucky: you all guys are making her things very complicated

Some where I also thinking that Ria is right, after the trip, i only cry while thinking about him maybe like he was vanished. After meeting with boss and doing my work, I asked only ria for tea.

We went down stair for drinking the tea; I asked her how I will stop my feelings for him. she give a great smile like she was happy that I listened to her, we were drinking a tea and she suddenly mentioned akash, she said 'i think, he is a perfect guy you should try her, you should go on a date with him, when I meet him, I really thought that he is perfect for you a handsome and hard working is absolutely perfect for you'

'no, I don't know want to try him, he is selfish and I want naina and akash to go on date'

'that naina, do you really think, her family allow to do love marriage; be practical, he is good just go on date with him, me and yash will arrange that'

'No....no...he is very boring'

'just one date, just one please; I will also there for examine him, if he will do anything boring, I will take you out from him'

'Alright, just one date'

'Yeah.. Just one date'

I was not satisfied with her answer, but she know very well how to convince me but I was thinking that why everyone want me to be with him, I did not even like him, not even we have matching choice.

Hour before date

I was being ready as my friend ria want to attach me with that damn akash, I don't know that how they asked akash for me to go on date that, I will definitely ask from him but the thing is what I will talk to him and what will I wear?. I don't have the massive choices, so, I just wear red dress again, I really look pretty good in that dress. My mom was very happy when she get to know that I am going on a date with akash, it makes her face become glow where my nani was bit upset, I get ready with my dress and little makeup on it.

I walk out from my room to look over Ria but she was standing in the door wearing very casual jeans and top and looking at me saying 'you are looking adorable', I smiled and she take me out of the house and akash was standing with the swift dezire with the sky blue t shirt and black trouser. He opened the door for me and made me sit on the front seat,

I was keep saying Ria to sit back on the car but she refused and said 'she will come with rickshaw'.

We both were sitting silently, silent music was going on as he love to listen silent music in car while driving and he asked me my favorite song and I tell him 'darasal' and all the memories were come into my end, all about mihir was going inside my brain, whatever he was saying , I was just saying 'hnn , hnnn' and ignoring everything he was saying.

We reached into the restaurant, take some drinks and stardom in first order, I telling him about the dum biryani, I eat in Kolkata and roll. He also started telling the dishes, he eat in his village, he tell me about the story about his village, when electricity went off and all the villagers were point out on his family sometime villager cut their electricity and they had to sleep in hot.

His conversation was not that much boring, it is very interesting, whenever I look at him, I thought that people can never say that he is born in village, he have a standard of talking, walking and everything, after all he is a perfect guy.

He asked me about mihir and vivek and I tell him that, how good my friendship was with then even now too. I shared every moment to him that I live in Kolkata, he was very happy to listen that.

The music was going on, people were dancing with their adorable couples and he asked me for dance and I did not refused, he take me to the dance floor and he said very fluently 'you are looking stunning' and I said 'you too', then I asked him that, how ria asked you to go on a date with me and he firstly and said 'that damn ria firstly called me and said with boldness you have to go on a date with saira and hang off the phone; I was scared with his tone, she did not asked me, she just tell me', the way he was telling the situation, I also laugh with him. Ria was also there looking at us laughing and thinking, she set it up very nicely [she is my best friend, I can read her mind]

We both were talking about many things, his experience, my experience about naina, mama and nani that think he is boring, I tell him this too, he is a chilled person, he never take things seriously, I don't want to say this but I really enjoying with him, I think him boring but when I meet him in person, I felt he is a good and interesting person.

It happens a late, so I tell him that I want to go home, so we both leave and sit on the car, we were become so much frank, so I take my phone and connect with speaker of his car and play good song accept 'darasal'.

Our homes are same, so we both entered in the home together, when I entered in the house , my mama was in a stress, I asked him, why she is upset and then she said 'amma is not well, she is having weakness and headache, I give her medicine, but she is still in pain' , I was become worried 'I tell you mama, buy blood pressure machine and it is night, how I will take her to clinic it is now 11 pm, you should call me mama'.

'I don't want to destroy your date'

'date is not important than nani'

Akash entered with purse in his hand and he said 'your purse was left, saira'. He also look into her faces and asked 'what happen; everything is alright?', I said 'nothing' and my mama said 'amma is not well, she is feeling weakness'

'maybe, it is a problem because of blood pressure, we should take her to doctor; she will be get fine till morning; we should not let this go'

I said 'yeah mama, akash is right'

'so you both go and take her'

Akash said 'where is nani?'

Akash grab the hand of nani and make her sit in his car and take us to clinic, unfortunately, clinic was closed, so he takes to the hospital and we got a doctor to look her. It was a lady doctor and she was too good. She checked the blood pressure of nani and said very calmly 'it is all normal, only blood pressure is decreased, I will give you blood pressure tablet she will be fine soon; nothing to worry about'.

It was too good to listen that everything is fine, when we back to our homes, I said him thank you for thank you and to help my family whatever I thought about him, it was all changed, whatever I think him that he is boring and all that, he was shy in people but when you meet him in person, he is damn interesting that moment while thinking about him somewhat I forget about Mihir maybe it is the sign to moved on from Mihir. At that night, I was thinking that, I should stop feeling for mihir and try thinking about akash. Ria was right mihir can only give me heart breaks and Akash is the easy going person, life would be easy with him and beautiful too.

After two days

Before leaving office at 5 p.m, the call came with unknown number, I did not look at the number seriously but then I pick up the call and it was mihir call 'hello saira'

'hey mihir, how you are doing?'

'I am good, you are in Meerut or travelling somewhere'

'it is just been 1 week for my Kolkata trip; it is not been year'

He laughed and said 'I hope; I did not disturbed you'

I said with 'no not at all'

'hey..i want to say something'

That time heart beating ten times better and he said with holding a silence 'I am coming meerut for some work'

I was a bit shocked that, meerut is a small city, how can someone have a work in this city and I said very confidently 'wait..you have work in this small city' with chuckling. 'yup..you are right it is a small city but the case is about a big robbery of electronics and we get a information that thieves are from Meerut'

'what a coincidence man; you are solving a meerut case, where I live'

'Actually, this was not my case, it is the case of Mr. Tripathi, he does not like travelling, so I request him to give this'

'so, you take the case for me'

'yeah..you can say'

'wow, so finally we are going to meet after weekend; I am very excited'

'yup..and what is going on in your life?'

'Yeah.. some tragedies are going on'

'what?'

'I will tell you, when we will meet; I don't like talking in phones'

'me too'

'so, bye; I will see you in meerut'

‘yup…bye’ and I end the call, I walk over to ria, unfortunately she was busy in meeting, so I text her ‘Mihir is here after week end’ and she replies ‘I will be in 10 minutes; wait for me’.

I was waiting for her and she took my fifteen minutes, and she came with very speed and shout ‘ what the heck; you were recovering from him and now he came and destroying everything’ I was putting my laptop and accessories in my bag and said ‘Ria you are overreacting, he take the case to meet me, maybe he want to meet me, maybe he also likes the way I like, I cannot stop him for meeting me or I cannot stop him liking me. If I will talk about myself, I am listening to you, I am trying liking akash but I cannot stop my feeling instantly; don’t worry we will come out from this very soon’. I walk away from my desk without saying any bye, she was still standing after entering in the elevator, she run toward me and entered in the elevator and hugged me and say with apologizing face ‘I am sorry, if I was putting pressure on you; I know you will come over very soon'.

I take the taxi, she also went off with another taxi, I was bit happy also and sorrow too. I was being happy because I will see him but the sad part for me was he will vanished again and that will hurt me again, when he will come, I should mostly ignored his things and did not let go for feelings.

I reached my home, I tell my mom and nani too that mihir will be come after the weekend, they were happy they want him to be stay with us, inside I was thinking, Ria was doing 100% to get over him and these guys are turning him with me. My family is too stupid, no one can ever guess there action.

After two days

It was a great Monday, I was being ready for going office and also waiting for mihir to come, he tell me that his flight will be land in 10 am and we were waiting for him from half hour, I call him, he said he is in taxi but who's know where they are, a bell rang I ran toward door. He was standing with his suitcase and wearing glasses, another guy were also there, so mama and I welcomed them my eyes were glowing while looking at him, I hugged very normally so, my mama never make judgment for hugging a man, we were both were smiling looking at each other face, we take them inside the house and make them comfortable with preserving water and snacks for them, I and mihir were talking very formally, how you are doing, what is your work and all that, he said they will stay only one day in meerut and next morning they will went off, I was being very late for office so, I tell him that I will meet him in evening, he also said he have some work and we both were agreed to meet in evening. Eventually, I promise him to do dinner with him.

I ran for my office and my boss was too angry to being so late but when you have the best colleagues, you never had to listen yelling statement. I tell them that mihir is staying tonight with our family and suddenly Ria have an idea, she said with begging eyes 'we all four will go on club and chill tonight till midnight, you will not have time to meet him and tomorrow he will went off; this is the best solution for ignoring him'.

'Fine..but I will back home at 10 please and this yash idiot will drop me'

Yash with making thumb 'done'

Ria said 'okay'

After office, we went to nearby pub, lucky already have the entrance pass, it was medusa pub, it was beautifully designed, there were many teenagers boys and girls were dancing and enjoying hilarious. I was enjoying too, because Ria was dancing very creepy whereas yash was drinking so much and he was talking about his ex and being sad. Me and lucky does not drink, so we were looking them, Ria take me to the dance floor and forcing me to dance with, I was refusing but I does not want to make her upset so, I also dance with him, I take Lucky with him and we four dancing very crazily, after drinking so much, yash was being so unmannered, he was just doing thing very hilarious, he also ask one woman to dance with him, who is very aged to him, looking at them was very funny, looking yash doing annoying give Ria confidence too, she also ask a boy to dance with him, and the boy was great dancer, he just fire on dance floor doing the most adorable moves. Ria become aside and watching him, people were hooding and shouting, It was being great time and then I realized, I promised Mihir for dinner, I run away from the pub while saying 'shit….bull shit…everything sucks',

I take taxi very fast and text Ria that 'I walk off from pub, don't worry', I was feeling very bad that, when I came to his city, he left all his work, just to make me explore everything, he just helped when, I was being stuck in police station, he is the only who just make my birthday too good and when it comes to me, I am just making him wait and breaking his promise. I was feeling very bad on myself, it was like please playback the time and I will spent my time with him.

When I reached to my area, my eyes were become red, the taxi driver drop me and he was standing in the roof and talking to his colleague and drinking coffee and I was staring him, because his messy hair were flying and it was long time since, I did not look his face while talking, and there was Akash and naina standing too, but I did not look at them as I was busy staring him, looking at him giving him another level of refreshment and they four of them starting laugh because I can see Mihir cracking his joke. Then, my eyes contact with him and he shout 'hey saira' before everyone look at me, I ran to up stair and my mama, hold my hand and said 'before going upstairs, wash your face and wear comfortable' then I thought, if I will argue with, definitely, she will be the one who will one and my time waste too so, I listened to her, with speed I wash my face and change my clothes. Then I run upstairs and there was no one and his colleague was outside and then he said 'he was very tired, he went to sleeping'.

I went inside to his room for see him and he was laying down very comfortably so, I walk away from home, while walking away, with googly voice he said 'hey saira', I turned my face with excitement, I looked at him with very regretting face, 'I am sorry; I am very sorry, I take so much time' and he said with laughing 'it is okay; you might be very busy', I cannot tell him that I was enjoying in pub, and I replied 'my boss make me sucked with many works'. He stands out and holds my hand and makes me walk away from and take me to roof and make me sit on cement chair 'I like your roof',

'Are you not angry with me?'

'I don't have time to angry with you'

I smiled looking towards his eyes and he said 'saira, I am sorry but I can't wait to tell you that "I like you"; I know that is so late but when you went back, I was just missing every second, every minute then I realized I fall for you, sing a song for you make me so happy, I don't hope for any relation from you but just I want to tell that I like and I always like you, It is okay if you did not like me back but, “I just like you; no one can stop me for this or I did not even know any reason to liking you”,

After listening his confession, it turns me blank, it turns me in surprised face, it turns me more complicated and then I get to remember everything about Ria that I had to move on and I had to move on and I said him with bit nervous ‘I respect your confession but the thing is “I like Akash” and I feel very sorry and don’t be sad everything will be pass soon; I am feeling very sleepy so, maybe I should go’, I take my first step to hugged him but he step back and he said with upset face ‘don’t hug me, I will cry; you should go’. I was looking his red eyes and he walk away without looking at me just give me smile and went back to his room and I was just looking his back and admiring him, I think, I give him the worst excuse as the person you like, like someone else is more heartbreaking than the person you like does not like you back.

I went to down stair ,where Akash live, I was being regretful, I want to do something that make me distracted from him, so I ring the bell of his door and akash came with wearing his nigh suit and said 'everything is okay' and I my eyes were become red and I said 'can we start dating', his expression was surprised with unconfirmed voice he said 'yeah…but' and he hold and said 'good night' and I walk away without even thinking what I said, without even listening to him, I silently entered in my house with looking everywhere that my mama is here or not and I entered in my room lock the door and started crying with holding my mouth shut and I went down on the floor, I was shedding tears while laying down on the floor, I did not know why I was crying on that damn night but I remember that I was feeling bad for the whole day. When I fall sleep on the floor, I never get to know, I was sleeping very deep that much that I never get to know, I stayed whole night lying down on the floor, when I wake up at 10 a.m I was having pain in my back, I cannot able to stand but I do some potential to stand.

Then I realized about night incident, I was started feeling bad but I did not cry, I unlocked the door and take a water bottle and my mother was cooking something and while I was drinking water she yelled and said ‘what happened to your eyes’ and I ran towards mirror and see that my eyes become swollen because of crying whole night, putting my hand on head I said ‘where is mihir and their colleague’ and she ignore my question and started asking the question about what happened at night, why your eyes become swollen and all that stuff and then I was become irritate and I screamed ‘where is mihir mama?’ and then she said with peaceful voice ‘he left the home at 8 am and he just informed me and leave’, with again irritate voice I said ‘ why did not you tell me?’ she said ‘your door was locked, I was knocking many times and then he leave without saying anything’. I was started feeling so bad again and I cannot able to blame anyone of them accept myself.

I get ready for my office, without eating anything, I went off from house and my mother started yelling at me about eat the breakfast and all that but I was bit tensed so; I went off without saying anything. When I reached my office all the three were talking about the pub night and then they saw me they give high five to me and they were talking that night was so hilarious and I was just giving them smile, Ria slap me on my back and asked 'why did you leave early', 'because it was too late my mama would killed me' I replied

Yash: you should asked me then, I will make you drop

Lucky: you cannot drop yourself on night, how would you drop her

They all were laughing and I was just smiling and Ria asked, is that mihir leave and tell her that he leave at 8 am without telling anyone accept mama, I cannot able to speak him even. She was being happy that I cannot speak to him, Ria was somewhere right but she was not understanding the feeling of mine and mihir.

I was doing my work and suddenly, my father do video call, I answered it and he said with honored eyes ‘how was your trip dear; and you idiot did not even tell me that you are going’ with chuckling I take my laptop in canteen area and replied ‘I am sorry dad; I will never repeat my mistake’

‘Kiddo, how you work is going on’

‘it is good and what is going in your love life’

‘Anne and I get divorced’

‘What!’ with loud, people look at me so I replied with low voice ‘what happened?’

‘I don’t want to talk about that stuff; I just called you because I was very happy that you go alone’

‘Yeah..’

‘How is your mama’

‘She is good, I think you and mom should patched up again’

He chuckled and said ‘that will never going to happen’ he hold and said ‘what you are doing this weekend’

I replied with smiling ‘nothing’

‘So, come to Delhi this weekend; I will wait for you’

‘Wait..how I can come’

‘because I am missing your bubbly face; I am booking the tickets’

‘Dad listen’

‘I did not want to listen anything; I am hanging off’

When my dad wants to meet me, he never listen any excuse, never listen to anyone, he just want to meet me anyhow, I know my dad very well, he was very disturbed due to the divorce so, he needs me to refreshment.

I was look in the window and think, this sorrow in my heart will be pass soon, to being hurt million times, it is good to be hurt for just one time.

It was happening evening, it was my time to leave the office, I give good bye to my friends and leave, I prefer to walk for miles because I did not getting any taxi, so I started walking and I remember the walk that me and mihir take and talk so nonsense, our debate is more in that nonsense, he always talk about his college and school memories.

I reached my home, there was Akash also coming from his office and then I realized the question, I asked him last night and I cover my face with bag and run, he was calling my name, so I stopped and said formally ‘what happened Akash?’, he come near and said ‘I was thinking about last time and then’ he holds and I said ‘may be my mama is calling me, I should go’ I run away and close the door of my house.

STURDAY MORNING

I was getting ready for going Delhi, my mom and nani again started the pooja in morning for my well wishing, they were again starting praying about my well journey, Delhi is just one hour far from meerut but still they were praying for my well journey, i was being ready with casual t shirt and jeans, I just carrying a one bag as I just want to stay there only one night.

We all three gather in breakfast table, eating Omelet and bread, my nani was bit upset as she does not like when I attach to my dad, and my mother felling a bit of insecurity, I see in their face as they were silently eating stuff and looking to the eyes of each other and then my mother said looking on the bread 'it will be better, if you not go to your dad'

'You know mama, I also don't want to go but he never listens when he wants to meet me'

They both again silently eating their stuff without saying anything, giving a sign to each other but before they will force me, I walk away from breakfast table and packing my accessories in my bag.

I leave the house at 9 a.m as my train was of 9;30, I was telling my mom that, that I will be fine as usual. I give them strong hug and taxi to train station.

I sit on the train, one family was also sit in other quarter and making fun of one of the young boy and sharing strong laugh and high fives, it was looking like, it is the get together after long time. I was looking at the window and thinking about the laugh we do when my mom and dad were together, the day when my nana come to home our home and he just only take me and spend the time only with me and ignore everything. Sometimes, things vanished very quickly that we cannot imagine.

After taking nap for so long, Train arrived in Delhi, sometimes I felt, Delhi is the type of city which carries many personalities, the people which opened mind and there are also people who still scared of various things, a city which carries many superstations and many crimes but the city also have its many advantage. My dad lives in karol bagh area and for that I need to go in metro station.

I arrived in karolbagh with metro even with rickshaw to and I called my dad about his locality, and it was not that much far from where my rickshaw stops me.

My dad was standing on his door, he was waving me, I run towards him and he hug me and say ‘I was missing you so much, kiddo’, he takes me to his apartment. The apartment was not much huge, it was build in so beautiful colony which carries many duplex, my dad was live in 2bhk, it was so huge for him even his apartment was well designed, he maintained the interior so beautiful. My dad is a hygienic man, his t-shirt always clean it never carries any single stain. His washroom and kitchen everything was so clean. He made me sit and give me a strawberry shake. When I was kid, I love to drink strawberry shake even the strawberry too. He made me realized that he never forget anything about me even he do three marriage too.

We were talking about my childhood stories, he talked about that he got promoted in his office. He talks about that how much toxic his Anne was and I was just listening and laughing the way he was explaining the stupidity about Anne then I tell him that my nani was unwell, one week before, he then asked about my mother with forgive eyes and I said 'she is good'

After talking with so much, at evening he cook a fantastic rajma chawal, the taste was awesome. He then shows me a picture of my childhood, he put them secretly, whenever he feel down, he always look at my picture and he gets refreshment.

The day was finished with talking so much, I was almost sleep then I heard the voice, from outside. So, I walk out from room and my dad was sitting on the kitchen floor, his eyes were become red. I walk towards him and he moved his head on another side and said 'what happened?',

'what happened; why you are crying dad?'

'hey kiddo, I am not crying'

'tell me dad; are you missing anne'

He look towards me and said 'yeah.. I am missing someone but not Anne but your mom'

'dad' I hold and he said 'I miss her, I don't even have the guts to say her that forgive me, I want to love with you'

I did not have idea that what will I said so he again said 'do you know, when me and your mom was in the college, she was the most popular girl in the college, the most beautiful girl, that every boy and girl want to be with her but she only loves me, still she only loves me; I remember that seven beautiful days, when we both got accused for bringing bottle of wine, we both got punishment for seven days, when everyone leaves, we both clean our classrooms and when I fall for him and when she fall for me, we both did not know'

'dad….it is okay'

'I regret so much saira; I miss that seven beautiful days'

My dad was feeling weak so much, I take him inside the room, he was very disturbed, then I realized, he search my mama in every woman, some mysterious was getting solved in my head that my mama know him very well that is the reason she never stops me to meet him. My dad maybe carries the pain of every woman, he cheated and then I realized they still love each other but they can never be together because of society and also of my father mistakes.

Whole night before sleeping, I was thinking about our four beautiful days. The way we both meet with misunderstanding, he helped me out from police station and we both explore the city together, eat every delicious menu to boating and cycling from birthday prank to singing a song for me. It was all four beautiful days, we live together. I was regretting that I did not say him that, I like him too, I was also regretting with my dad, I like someone who likes me too but I am listening that damn Ria who did not even understand the feeling, to share my pain, I get to my dad, he was looking at the picture of my mom, I knock the door and he wipe up his tears.

I enter in his room and sit very comfortably in his breathe, I take deep breath and said 'I like someone'

He chuckled and said 'seriously, who is that lucky man'

I smiled and said 'it was that Mihir, who helps me in kolkata'

He stroke his hand on my hairs and said 'kiddo, you grow so much, now you are dating someone'

I said with blushing 'naah…it is not like that'

He become shocked and said 'that idiot does not like you'

'he likes me but….' I hold and he said 'tell me everything clearly'

'I like him, he like me too but one of my colleague that is Ria, I tell her that, I like him and she brain washed me with saying that he will hurt me and when he said he likes me, so I said that I like akash that lives in our house'

'it is a huge messed up; saira'

'Yeah…I know and now I am regretting, he did not talk me, I want to talk him; I want to spend time with him also I want to know more about him'

'You are so loser in feelings'

'Don't make me feel bad, give me advice'

'when I said your mother about my feeling, I just said and did not think about anything, I just said him; for you I will only give advice, if you want to do regret like me so, just continue with this and if you don't want and you seriously like him then just buckle up and run to Kolkata and apologized him if he loves you, he will definitely forgive you'

I was gone in deep thoughts and he hold for some time and said ‘I want to sleep; you have a whole night to think now go to your room’

I move back to my room and thinking about whole night only one sentence, he said and then after being almost sleep, I found out the conclusion that I have to go to Kolkata and confessed everything so then I booked the tickets for morning flight to Kolkata, I was lucky that one seat was left.

Hour before flight

I was being ready, doing packing my stuff , my dad wakes up knock to my door and said ‘good morning kiddo; where are you going’ and I said with smile ‘I take decision to meet to one who’s name is always in my head’. He chuckled and walk into me and kissed in my forehead and said ‘I proud of you kiddo; I am making breakfast eat and go fast’

He made me a sandwich, he was excited more than me, he was helping me doing packing my stuff, ordering me not to forget my bag and the money and call him every minute, we both make a deal to not say anything to my mama. He drops me in airport do documentary things and leave.

My stomach was paining like butterflies in the stomach punching; I was somewhere happy and nervous too. I was thinking Kolkata, is so beautiful city for me. After thinking about mihir and mihir, listening music, and taking nap. I arrived in Kolkata with beautiful smile in my face. This time it was my little bag and I look at the time as it was weekend but I know him, he was busy in office and this time, I took rickshaw and give them the address that I remember almost.

His office was so far from airport. I change two rickshaws in hot weather. He stopped me from ten meter away from his office, I walk to his office, when I take the elevator, I was hoping that he will be there. I entered in his office, I look everywhere but he was not there, then suddenly someone knock on my Back and it was Prateek, he said 'hello…..' with big smile and i ignore his smile and I said 'where he is', and he said 'he is gone somewhere for investigation, he will come after one hour' and I said with loud 'why this stupid man always vanished when I want him' then everyone look at me then prateek was like 'do you want water; if you want I will drop you in Red diary café or you can sit here' I was in so angry mood so I prefer to sit and wait for him.

It was happened one hour and still he was not here, I was waiting and looking on the clock , people were preserving me coffee and saying that they will drop me in Red diary café but I just want to wait for him, it comes to happen evening, they were again offer me tea and biscuit. Then after long time when it almost happened to be night, he arrived with two police officers talking and holding the file in his hand. I look at him and he was just talking with them and shaking their hands and give him a file and give a signal for bye. He shouts very loud and said ‘I want a tea’ then he looked me and I looked at him. He was a bit shocked while looked at me, we both were gazing each other for so long then he came to me and said ‘why you are here?, Is everything is good’ with so caring voice. I said with nervous ‘I want to say something’, and then he said with clearing his throat ‘what?’, ‘I did not think, this is the good place to say something’

He hold my hand and take me to the downstairs where it is the beautiful garden, he make me sit on the bench, the sky was become orange, the stars were brightening so little and the grass was looking so greener and then with closing the eyes and with the deep breath I said ‘from the day you helped to the night when you surprised me, I was extremely fall for you but when you said that you like me, I was a bit confused about is our relation will be healthy or filled with various pain but when I meet my dad then I feel how much it is heartbreaking of losing your love’ I hold and he said ‘I don’t like carries a relationship,

I did not even believe in marriages but I believe in togetherness a person who never leave you and I also believe you are that person who just always be with me even we are far away with many miles'. I look into his eyes and I said 'I leave everything behind me, the people who were forcing me to be with Akash, I ignored them as I want to be with you for ever after'. He hugged me and I was thinking being with someone who makes you comfortable and calm,is always the great person. That time, I promised myself that I will make my mom and dad together again at anyhow.

www.ingramcontent.com/pod-product-compliance
Lightning Source LLC
LaVergne TN
LVHW041104150826
845673LV00007B/1926

9798756156263